Violin I

SCHIRMER'S LIBRARY
OF MUSICAL CLASSICS

GIOVANNI BATTISTA VIOTTI

Duets
For Two Violins

Edited by

LEOPOLD LICHTENBERG

ISBN 978-0-7935-5113-2

G. SCHIRMER, Inc.

DISTRIBUTED BY

HAL•LEONARD®
CORPORATION
7777 W. BLUEMOUND RD. P.O. BOX 13819 MILWAUKEE, WI 53213

Ⴈ Down bow
V Up bow
Nt Nut
M. Middle
Pt Point
Edited by Leopold Lichtenberg.

Six Duets.

VIOLIN I.

G. B. Viotti. Op. 20.

Moderato risoluto.

Printed in the U.S.A. by G. Schirmer, Inc.

14892a

Minore.

D Maggiore.

Violin II

SCHIRMER'S LIBRARY
OF MUSICAL CLASSICS

Giovanni Battista Viotti

Duets
For Two Violins

Edited by

LEOPOLD LICHTENBERG

ISBN 0-7935-5113-7

G. SCHIRMER, Inc.

DISTRIBUTED BY

7777 W. BLUEMOUND RD. P.O. BOX 13819 MILWAUKEE, WI 53213

Edited by Leopold Lichtenberg.

Six Duets.

VIOLIN II.

G. B. Viotti. Op. 20.

⊓　Down bow.
Ⅴ　Up bow.
Nt.　Nut.
M.　Middle.
Pt.　Point.

Moderato risoluto.

11892ᵇ

Printed in the U.S.A. by G. Schirmer, Inc.

VIOLIN II.

VIOLIN II.

Fine.

Menuetto Da Capo

14892b

14892b

VIOLIN II.

Trio.

A

B

Menuetto Da Capo.

14892b

14892

Fine.

Trio.

Menuetto D. C.

148929

148923

14892a

Allegretto.

148929